# SACRED TIME
## THE JEWISH CALENDAR AND LIFE CYCLE

By Judy Dick

BEHRMAN HOUSE
www.behrmanhouse.com

Design: Terry Taylor Studio
Editorial Committee: Ellen J. Rank, Diane Zimmerman

Copyright © 2012 Behrman House, Inc.
Published by Behrman House, Inc.
Springfield, NJ 07081
www.behrmanhouse.com

ISBN: 978-0-87441-863-7

Printed in the United States of America

**The publisher gratefully acknowledges the following sources of photographs and graphic images:**
(T=top, B=bottom, L=left, R=right)
Alanna E. Cooper 23; Alberto Jona Falco 30; Israel Ministry of Tourism 37T; Tobi Kahn, Natyh 23; Rachel Katzir 36 k'tubah; Richard Lobell 13 siddur, 13 Havdalah, 13 spices; Debbie Schopf 37B; Shutterstock: Golden Pixels LLC (cover family, 1), Ekaterina Lin (cover hupah, 34, 35 middle, 36 hupah), Yuri Samsonov (cover candle, 42T), Mikhail Tchkheidze (cover newborn, 20), Konstantin Goldenberg (cover Torah scroll), DenisNata 2L, Dima Sobko 2 middle, Valeriy Lebedev 2R, Pete Pahham 3L, Sergey Lavrentev 3 middle, Gelpi 3R, Rob Hainer 4TL, Lisa F. Young 4TR, 31, 33, iofoto 4BL, Yaro 4BR, Rasulov 5TL, Morgan Lane Photography 5TR, ChameleonsEye 5BL, pat138241 6 crying, Yuri Arcurs 6 dancing, Sergiy Bykhunenko 6 silence, Andrey Shadrin 6 laughing, Iakov Filimonov 6 planting, Kati Neudert 8, Mikhail Levit 9, Noam Armonn 10, 19 eating matzah, 19 waving flags, Joe Seer 11, S1001 12T, Dean Gah 12B, pavelr 13 Kiddush cup, 36 Kiddush cup, Korionov 14, Rafael Pacheco 15, Ingrid Prats 17, Elzbieta Sekowska 19 hamantashen, Yosefer 19 girl in costume, Glam 19 Holocaust symbol, Elena Schweitzer 21, OLJ Studio 25, Rob Swanson 26, Luba 27T, infografick 27B, Rozaliya 28, Teerapun 29, york777 35T, Stavchansky Yakov 35B, Aleksandar Bunevski 36 camera, Julia Ivantsova 36 women's shoes, 36 pen, Andrew Duany 36 centerpiece, Sergey Sklezenev 36 glass, Keith Levit 36 siddur, kuleczka 36 rings, Zakharoff 36 men's shoes, Rob Marmion 38T, Thomas M Perkins 38 middle, Jaren Jai Wicklund 38B, Arkady Mazor 39, lumen-digital 40, David Rabkin 42B, Ivan Montero Martinez 43, Dmitriy Shironosov 47, Photosindiacom LLC 48; Yeshiva University Museum 22 Torah binder (wimpel) of Shmuel ben Yaakov (Michael Sam Reinheimer) Painter: Rev. Reuben M. Eschwege (1890-1977), New York, 1946, Ink and gouache on cotton, Collection of Yeshiva University Museum, New York (1994.166), Gift of Mr. And Mrs. Michael Reinheimer; Jeffrey Zablow 42 middle.

**The publisher wishes to acknowledge the following source for quotes:**
Soomekh, page 11: courtesy of BabagaNewz.

Library of Congress Cataloging-in-Publication Data

Dick, Judy.
 Sacred time : the Jewish calendar and life cycle / by Judy Dick.
    p. cm. — (Building Jewish identity ; v. 2)
  ISBN 978-0-87441-863-7
1. Judaism—Customs and practices—Juvenile literature.  2. Jewish calendar—Juvenile literature.  3. Time—Religious aspects—Judaism—Juvenile literature.  4. Fasts and feasts—Judaism—Juvenile literature.  5 Life cycle, Human—Religious aspects—Judaism—Juvenile literature.  I. Title.
  BM700.D484 2012
  296.4'3--dc23
                                    2012010199

# CONTENTS

# CHAPTER 1

# TIMES OF YOUR LIFE

Your first day of school, a family seder, and a vacation at the beach...your memories are like snapshots in an album. We try to capture precious moments by taking photos and videos, but what are other ways to make events in your life memorable?

# Appreciating Every Minute

Jewish tradition does not let time pass without our paying attention to the moment. We are taught that each moment in our lives is important, and therefore, we have a Jewish calendar and life-cycle events to mark the times of our lives in a meaningful way. Our special rituals make Jewish holidays and life-cycle events unforgettable. Take a look at the photos on these pages, for example. Each shows a special moment in someone's life. Look closely at what each person is doing and try to identify how and when the event is being celebrated. Write your answers under each photo.

What photo from your own family's Jewish celebrations would you add? Print out a copy of it and paste it here.

# To Everything There Is a Season

The Torah itself teaches us to be aware of the passing of time and celebrate important moments, beginning with its account of each day of Creation. We read how our ancestors valued life-cycle events, like the birth of a new baby, and learn that observance of Jewish holidays, along with their rituals, are *mitzvot* to be kept by **Am Yisrael**, the Jewish people, throughout history. The Torah's message is that time is **sacred**, or holy and spiritual. We should appreciate the holiness of human life during its high and low moments.

One way to look at time is expressed beautifully in the Book of Ecclesiastes. Ecclesiastes was written by the wise King Solomon, the third king of Israel.

**A season is set for everything, a time for every experience under heaven: A time to be born and a time to die, a time to plant and a time to uproot the planted; a time to kill and a time to heal, a time to destroy and a time to build; a time to cry and a time to laugh, a time to mourn and a time to dance; … a time to tear and a time to sew, a time to keep quiet and a time to speak; a time to love and a time to hate; a time for war and a time for peace.** (Ecclesiastes 3:1–8)

# Jewish Times

King Solomon's words also relate to the Jewish calendar and life-cycle events. When is it time to do each of these things? Match each activity to the appropriate Jewish times. Each item may have more than one match.

1. Yom Ha'atzma'ut
(Israel Independence Day)

2. Simḥat Torah

3. Jewish funeral

4. Jewish wedding

5. Brit milah/brit bat
(celebrating the birth of a baby)

6. Bar/bat mitzvah

7. Tisha B'Av
(fast day commemorating the destruction of the First and Second Temples)

8. Tu BiShevat

# Noting New Experiences

One special way that Jews mark the passage of time is through prayer. For example, we say the *Sheheḥeyanu* blessing, or **b'rachah**, to express our thankfulness to God for new or uncommon experiences.

בָּרוּךְ אַתָּה יְיָ אֱלֹהֵינוּ מֶלֶךְ הָעוֹלָם, שֶׁהֶחֱיָנוּ וְקִיְּמָנוּ וְהִגִּיעָנוּ לַזְּמַן הַזֶּה.

**Baruch Atah Adonai Eloheinu Melech ha'olam sheheḥeyanu v'kiy'manu v'higi'anu laz'man hazeh.**

**"Praised are You, Adonai our God, Ruler of the world, who has given us life, sustained us, and enabled us to reach this time."**

Here are some examples of opportunities to say this blessing. Write a personal memory for as many examples as you can.

On wearing new clothes: _____

On using something for the first time: _____

On tasting a fruit that you haven't eaten in a long time: _____

On celebrating the first night of a Jewish holiday: _____

On seeing a friend for the first time in a year: _____

## Your Turn

Now add your own verse to those of King Solomon. Think of opposite pairs of "times" to add to King Solomon's text.

A time to _____ and

   a time to _____

A time to _____ and

   a time to _____ .

## Talk about It

What are some ways that time can be sacred or holy? How can Jewish rituals turn an ordinary day into an extraordinary one?

# CHAPTER 2

# MAKING TIME FOR THE JEWISH WEEK

**Did you know that the Jewish day begins when the sun sets? Or that the Hebrew names of the days of the week are actually numbers? In fact, Shabbat is the only day that has a name that is not a number. What do you think this says about how we view the weekdays in relation to Shabbat?**

## All in a Week's Work

By the time you wake up in the morning, a good part of your Jewish day is over because it began the evening before. This way of keeping time dates back to the creation of the world. In the account of Creation in the Torah, the Bible describes that each day first had an evening, which then was followed by the morning. This is also why Shabbat and Jewish holidays begin in the evening.

Why do you think that evening came before morning in each day of Creation? Do you think this system of time makes sense? Why or why not? _____

_____

The names of the days of the week also come from the Torah. The first day of the Jewish week, Sunday, is called *Yom Rishon,* which means just that—"first day"! The next day's name is *Yom Sheini,* "second day," named after the second day of creation. Each name followed, as all the work of Creation was finished.

### Words to Know:
**shavu'a, sheva**

In Hebrew, a week is called **shavu'a**. It is based on the Hebrew word for seven, **sheva**. So a week, made up of seven days, gets its name from a number too.

# Counting the Days and Making Them Count

Write down the English translation and the secular day of the week under each of the Hebrew days of the week. The first one has been done for you. Then think about the Jewish actions you do at each given time. Being Jewish isn't something we do only on Shabbat. There are mitzvot that you can do every day. Write your ideas into your planner below. Some examples are filled in for you.

| | Morning | Afternoon | Evening |
|---|---|---|---|
| Yom Rishon "First Day" Sunday | Turn off the light when leaving a room. | | |
| Yom Sheini _____ _____ | | | |
| Yom Sh'lishi _____ _____ | | Call a friend who is sick. | |
| Yom R'vi'i _____ _____ | | | |
| Yom Ḥamishi _____ _____ | | | Recite the Sh'ma before going to sleep. |
| Yom Shishi _____ _____ | | | |

# Hebrew Time

This watch has Hebrew letters in place of numbers. Each Hebrew letter of the alphabet is also a number. For example, a *bet*, the second letter in the Hebrew alphabet, is also the number 2.

What Hebrew letter represents one o'clock? _____

What time is represented by the letter *vav*? _____

Copy the Hebrew letters that represent twelve o'clock. _____

# A Shabbat State of Mind

Each day of the week is valuable, but in Jewish life the time we wait for all week is Shabbat. As we go through each weekday, the final count builds up to the last day. We have all kinds of rituals and customs that turn Shabbat into something extraordinary: lighting candles, special blessings and songs, joyful meals with family and friends, and meaningful synagogue services.

# Shabbat in the Torah

Why is the last day of the week so special to Am Yisrael? The answer can be found in Kiddush, the blessing said on Shabbat over wine or grape juice to sanctify (make holy or special) the holy day and to set it apart from the rest of the weekdays. Part of the Kiddush comes from the Torah.

> **And it was evening and it was morning, the sixth day. The heaven and earth were completed and all their array. On the seventh day God finished the work that God had been doing, and God rested on the seventh day from all God's work which God had done. And God blessed the seventh day and declared it holy, because on it God had rested from all the work of creation which God had done.**
> **(Genesis 1:31–2:3)**

What biblical story is this about? _____

In this story, what made the seventh day different from all the other days of the week? _____

_____

How can you create rest in your life? _____

Later in the Torah, Am Yisrael was given the mitzvah of celebrating Shabbat:

> **Remember the Sabbath day and keep it holy.** (Exodus 20:8)

What does it mean to remember Shabbat? _____

What are ways that we can keep Shabbat holy? _____

# Greetings

On Shabbat, Jews greet each other by saying "Shabbat Shalom!" Practice writing the Hebrew words Shabbat Shalom in the speech bubbles.

שַׁבָּת שָׁלוֹם

## Words to Know:
### Kiddush, Shabbat

The word **Kiddush** comes from the Hebrew word for holy, *kadosh*. Kadosh means to make something special by making it different and connected to God. The word **Shabbat** means "rest." Resting from work and going to services on Shabbat are some ways to make the day different and connected to God.

## Meet Bahar Soomekh

**Actress Bahar Soomekh describes how she feels about Shabbat:**

I love Shabbat. When Wednesday or Thursday rolls around, I feel peace in my heart knowing that Shabbat is coming and I can disconnect from the world. Shabbat is time to connect with my family and God, and to appreciate life. I don't take Shabbat for granted.

**What can you add to your Shabbat observance so you don't take Shabbat for granted?**

# Only the Best for Shabbat

One way to make Shabbat extra special is to save our best and most beautiful things for Shabbat. Keeping our most beautiful clothing or the most delicious foods and drink for the festive Shabbat meals are some examples of *hidur mitzvah*, making the mitzvah of Shabbat extra beautiful. There are even items that are made especially for Shabbat, like ḥallah, the special Shabbat bread, which usually comes in a braided shape. Today you can buy ḥallah in all kinds of flavors: raisin, garlic, whole wheat and honey, even chocolate chip! Which is your favorite?

# All Set for Shabbat

Set the table for Shabbat in style by drawing a Shabbat meal of your own design. You can choose items from the word bank to put on the table, or add things that are not listed (like people).

**Word Bank:** Kiddush cup, flowers, ḥallah, grape juice, plates, napkins, ḥallah cover, salt shaker, Shabbat candles, glasses, siddur, tablecloth, soup, spoons, cake, ḥallah plate

# Endings and Beginnings

Just as there are special rituals at the beginning of Shabbat, there is also a special ceremony at its end: *havdalah*. Havdalah means "separation." The ceremony includes blessings over wine, fragrant spices, and a special candle flame. It ends with a b'rachah, blessing, thanking God for separating the holy from the everyday.

# Shavu'a tov!  Have a good week!

The havdalah ceremony uses all our senses and gives us energy for the coming week. Match each havdalah object to its correct sense by writing the number of the answer below each object.

1. Smell: we smell spices to bring the sweet scent of Shabbat into the week.

2. Hearing: we say or hear the havdalah blessings.

3. Touch: we hold the siddur and read the words of the havdalah.

4. Sight: we look at the flames to remind us of the separation of darkness and light, holy and everyday.

5. Taste: we drink the wine or grape juice.

## Talk about It

"More than the Jews have kept Shabbat, Shabbat has kept the Jews," said the writer Ahad Ha'am. What do you think he meant? How can celebrating Shabbat help strengthen our Jewish identity?

# CHAPTER 3

# CELEBRATING THE JEWISH YEAR

**In today's world, we turn to calendars and clocks for the date and time. But the passing of time is also marked by the cycles of the sun and the moon.**

## Legendary Moon

According to Jewish legend, the sun and the moon, the two great lights, were created the same size. However, the moon complained to God that just as two kings cannot wear one crown, the sun and the moon cannot both be equal in size. God listened and then made the moon smaller. The moon was very upset and cried out again to God. To calm the moon down, God promised that Am Yisrael would determine its calendar by the moon. God also gave the stars to the moon as friends for all time.

## Phases of the Moon

Last Day of the Jewish Month

15th Day

Rosh Hodesh: First Day of the Jewish Month

# Good Night Moon

We already learned that a Jewish day begins in the evening and that seven Jewish days make up the Jewish week, which ends in Shabbat. Jewish months also have their own names and features. Just like the secular calendar (the calendar you use in your everyday life), the Jewish calendar has twelve months, but each Hebrew month is determined by the cycles of the moon. Each month is twenty-nine or thirty days long, the time it takes for the moon to revolve around the Earth. We begin a Jewish month on **Rosh Ḥodesh**, the day when we see the sliver of a new moon in the sky. In ancient times, the month was not recognized until witnesses confirmed that they saw the new moon. Today, we use a fixed calendar that has already calculated the cycles of the moon.

If you look for the new moon on Rosh Ḥodesh, you will see that it looks like a narrow crescent. As the month continues, you will see more and more of the moon, until on the fifteenth of the month, the full moon can be seen in the night sky. After this, the moon starts to look smaller again. When we see this, we know that a Jewish month is ending and a new one will soon begin.

## Your Turn

For one month, watch the moon and record how its appearance changes. Make a calendar page with the Hebrew dates of all the days in the month and enough room for images of the moon. Each night, sketch the moon in the correct box on your calendar. When you see the new moon and the full moon, make a note next to your sketch for that evening.

## Words to Know:
### Rosh Ḥodesh

The first day of each Jewish month is called **Rosh Ḥodesh**, which literally means the "head of the month." The Hebrew word *ḥodesh* is related to the word *ḥadash*, which means "new." What does this teach you about how we view each month?

# Keeping Track of Two Calendars

Although Jewish holidays occur at the same time each year on the Hebrew calendar, the dates they correspond to on the secular calendar change each year. This is because the secular calendar is based on the rotation of the earth around the sun, while our Jewish calendar is determined by the rotation of the moon around the earth. Since the cycles of the moon and the sun don't match up exactly, the two calendars do not match up exactly either. In fact, the Jewish calendar is about eleven days shorter than the secular calendar.

In order to keep the holidays of the Jewish calendar lined up with the seasons of the solar year, we add an extra month to the Jewish calendar in certain years. The Jewish leap year, therefore, has thirteen months, with an extra month of Adar. But this doesn't mean that we celebrate Purim twice! Instead, Purim is saved for the second Adar.

# It's About Time

Complete your own Jewish calendar. Below you'll find a list of ways to get ready for the Jewish holidays. Write the name of each holiday on the calendar on the facing page, in the correct Hebrew month. Find out the date of your Hebrew birthday and add it in the correct month too.

1. Eat fruit from Israel on Tu BiShevat, the New Year of the Trees, on the 15th of Shevat.

2. Hear the shofar on Rosh Hashanah, the Jewish New Year, on the first and second days of Tishre.

3. Buy candles to light the Ḥanukkah menorah, beginning on the 25th of Kislev.

4. Bake *hamantashen* as a tasty treat for Purim, celebrated on the 14th of Adar.

5. Choose a haggadah to use at the Passover seder, on the 15th of Nisan.

6. Wave an Israeli flag on Yom Ha'aztma'ut, Israel's Independence Day, on the 5th of Iyar.

7. Prepare a filling meal to eat before the Yom Kippur fast, the 10th of Tishre.

8. Study the Ten Commandments on Shavuot, on the 6th of Sivan.

9. Build and decorate a sukkah by the 15th of Tishre, just in time for Sukkot.

10. Remember the destruction of the Temples in Jerusalem on the fast of Tisha B'Av, the 9th of Av.

11. Dance with a Torah on Simḥat Torah, on the 22nd of Tishre.

12. Remember the Jews who lost their lives in the Holocaust on Yom Hashoah, the 27th of Nisan.

**Tishre**
September–October

**Ḥeshvan**
October–November

**Kislev**
November–December

**Tevet**
December–January

**Shevat**
January–February

**Adar**
February–March

**Nisan**
March–April

**Iyar**
April–May

**Sivan**
May–June

**Tammuz**
June–July

**Av**
July–August

**Elul**
August–September

**Words to Know:** shanah

The Hebrew word for year, *shanah*, is included in the name of one of the most important Jewish holidays, **Rosh Hashanah**, which means "the head of the year." The Hebrew word for change, *shinui*, is related to the word *shanah*. What does this teach you about the Jewish view of time?

# Celebrate Good Times!

Everybody has their favorite times of year. Some kids, for example, can't wait to put on their winter coats and boots and jump into the snow, while others look forward to seeing the first blossoms of spring. Some dream of summer all year long, while others look forward to the crisp air of fall. We each have our favorite Jewish times of year, too. Do you prefer singing the prayers in the synagogue on Rosh Hashanah or attending family gatherings on Ḥanukkah? Take this quiz to find out your "Jewish holiday personality."

## Giving It Your All for the Jewish Holidays

For each question, circle the answer that best describes what you do or what you would like to do.

1. **You prepare for the High Holidays by:**
   a. Giving tzedakah to your favorite charity.
   b. Asking forgiveness from your friends and family.
   c. Learning how to blow a shofar.

2. **Your family is building a sukkah this year. Your parents ask you to help them get it ready, so you:**
   a. Spend all day building it with them.
   b. Figure out how to set up the table and chairs so that everyone will be comfortable.
   c. Study the holiday Kiddush and other blessings for Sukkot so you can say them for everyone.

3. **As Ḥanukkah approaches, what role do you play in the festivities?**
   a. Practice the Ḥanukkah candle-lighting blessings so you can light your own Ḥanukkah menorah this year.
   b. Get really involved in planning the presents you will give to your family.
   c. Help plan your class's Ḥanukkah party so it's the best one ever.

4. **The best part of your religious school's Tu BiShevat party was:**
   a. Tasting all the new fruits from Israel.
   b. Spending time outdoors with friends.
   c. Taking charge of a recycling project.

5. **You think your class's Purim party was great because of:**
   a. The dramatic retelling of the Purim story you organized.
   b. The delicious foods contributed by each family that joined, including your special hamantashen.
   c. The crazy costumes that everyone wore, which were based on a theme you suggested.

6. **At the Passover seder, you:**
   a. Rush to hide (or find) the *afikoman*, reenact the plagues, and open the door to welcome Elijah the Prophet.
   b. Keep busy helping to pass out the matzah and other special foods at the seder.
   c. Sing all the Passover songs and blessings out loud, including the Four Questions.

**7. When your school prepares for Yom Ha'atzma'ut, your favorite part is:**
   a. Waving your blue-and-white Israeli flag.
   b. Learning how Jewish people from all over the world come together in Israel.
   c. Leading the singing of Israel's national anthem "Hatikvah."

**Calculate your score. How many of each letter did you circle?**

a: _____   b: _____   c: _____

**If you circled:**

   **Mostly a's: Go-Getter:** You like to take action to make every holiday great. Whether it's getting up there and performing or enthusiastically doing the holiday rituals, you have it covered.

   **Mostly b's: Giver:** You like to make the holidays special for your friends and family. Their interests are always at the center of what you do, and you look forward to holiday gatherings all year.

   **Mostly c's: Holiday Director:** You love to lead everyone in Jewish holiday traditions. Eager to teach and confident in your knowledge of the traditions, you are a great help at school and at home.

Does this sound like you? How would you describe your "Jewish holiday personality" in your own words?

_____

_____

_____

## Talk about It

During the year, how can you make the best use of time? How would you describe to a friend the Jewish concept of time?

# CHAPTER 4

# THE FIRST STEPS IN A JEWISH LIFE

Do you remember your first Passover? How was it different from your last one? You can measure your growth by remembering how you have changed as you celebrate the same holiday year after year. Just as we mark important times of the year with Jewish rituals, we also have meaningful ways to celebrate major events in our lives.

## A New Jewish Life

The birth of a Jewish baby is cause for great celebration. At a **brit milah**, the Jewish circumcision ceremony, a newborn baby boy is welcomed into the Jewish community after his first week of life. Friends and family bless the baby saying, " *... may he enter into Torah study, marriage, and good deeds.* " Another ceremony, called the **brit bat**, celebrates the birth of a baby girl.

# Kicking Off a New Jewish Life

A new baby is an addition not only to a family, but also to the Jewish nation. The ceremonies that celebrate a birth are also the first steps that set a Jewish child on the path to a Jewish life. The brit milah ceremony for a baby boy has a long history, while the celebrations for a baby girl are both more recent and more diverse. One important feature of these ceremonies is giving the baby a Jewish name.

## It's a Boy!

Did you know that a brit milah is the first Jewish life-cycle event mentioned in the Torah? Abraham circumcised his son Isaac on the eighth day after Isaac was born, just as God had commanded. This is why the brit milah is usually held on the eighth day of a baby's life.

Do you remember the *Brit*, the agreement, made between Abraham and God and renewed at Mount Sinai between God and Am Yisrael? When God gave Abraham the mitzvah of brit milah, which means the covenant (agreement) of circumcision (removing the foreskin), it was meant to be a physical sign of the unique relationship between God and the Jewish nation.

## It's a Girl!

While the brit milah ceremony for a baby boy has a long history and a specific order, many of the ways to celebrate a baby girl's birth are newer and more diverse. One of the oldest traditions is to announce a baby girl's Hebrew name at the Torah reading in synagogue shortly after her birth. Today, many families also perform other rites at the brit bat (covenant of the daughter), or *simḥat bat* (rejoicing over a daughter) ceremony, such as lighting candles, having a festive meal, announcing her name, and reciting special texts and blessings.

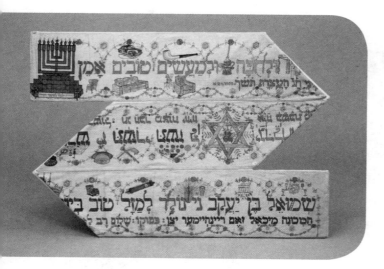

# A Welcome Tradition

Using a Torah binder, also known as a *wimpel*, is a unique custom of some Eastern European Jewish communities that ties together the ceremony of brit milah or brit bat with future Jewish life-cycle events. The wimpel was made from the cloth a baby was wrapped in at the brit milah or brit bat ceremony.

The design on this wimpel includes the baby's name, a blessing with good wishes for his future, and illustrations of Jewish holiday rituals. The binder is wrapped around a Torah scroll later in the child's life when he or she is called to read the Torah as a bar or bat mitzvah and again before his or her wedding. This particular Torah binder was personalized with decorations relating to the baby's life. A wimpel is like a timeline of a baby's future. What would a timeline of your past and future life look like?

# Honoring Special Moments

Artist Tobi Kahn designs his own ceremonial pieces for his family events. "It's important to honor special moments in life. By creating ceremonial objects, you are an active participant in the ritual." When his daughter was born, he designed these chairs for the ceremony at which she received her name. The chairs served as special seats from which the baby's mother and grandmothers welcomed the new female member of the family.

# Meet Rebecca

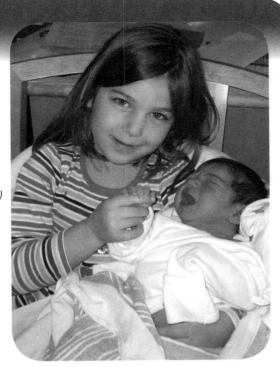

**Lives in: Boston, Massachussets**

*When her baby sister was born, Rebecca was able to say her own prayer for the baby at the simḥat bat. Together with her sister Anna Belle, she said: "Our sister, may you be the mother of thousands of ten thousands."* (Genesis 24:60)

**When My Baby Sister Was Born:** I remember going to the hospital, and she looked like a cute baby. I was very happy, and I liked to hold her.

**Memories from My Sister's Simḥat Bat:** I remember sitting in the front with my cousins and looking at the little baby. There were a lot of people there—my cousins, some of my friends, my aunts and uncles and my grandparents. My grandma held the baby when she got her name. My aunt announced her name, Miriam!

**My Jewish Life:** I go to a Jewish Community Day School. I'm in second grade. In first grade I learned Hebrew and *t'filot* (prayers) and how to read and to do math. We also learned the stories of the *Avot* (forefathers) and *Imahot* (foremothers). My favorite holiday is Passover because I usually get to see my cousins and my grandparents and I like to eat eggs dipped in salt water during the seder.

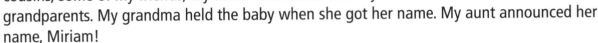

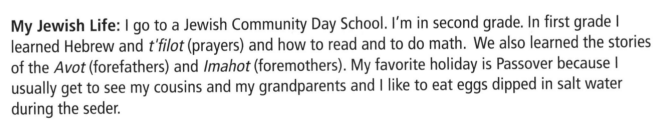

## More Than One Path to a Jewish Life

When babies are adopted, their birth parents may not be Jewish, and so they get a Hebrew name after undergoing a conversion ceremony to become Jewish. In addition to the brit milah or brit bat ceremony, these babies may also get a dip in the *mikvah*, a ritual pool of water, and are joyously welcomed into the Jewish nation. They are called converts because they converted (changed) to Judaism. Abraham and Sarah, the first Jews, are considered a convert's Jewish parents. One of the most famous converts in our history was Ruth, a greatly admired biblical heroine.

# What's in a Name?

Choosing a Hebrew name for a baby takes thought. Some parents name a child after a deceased relative. Others choose a biblical name or another Jewish name from the past. Another popular choice is to give the baby a name that has a significant meaning or relates to the time of year the child was born. A Hebrew name is not just a label or a way to identify a person, it is a reflection of the kind of person we would like the child to be. The child's Hebrew name will be used in the future at other life-cycle ceremonies, such as at his or her bar or bat mitzvah and wedding, and each time the person is called for an honor *(aliyah)* to the Torah.

# Biblical Names

The Hebrew names of these biblical personalities all have special meanings. Match each Hebrew name to the correct Hebrew word, with the help of these biblical quotes. Circle the Hebrew letters that are shared by each name and its related meanings.

**"The man called his wife's name Eve, because she had become the mother of all the living."** (Genesis 3:20)

**"Then his brother emerged, holding on to the heel of Esau; so they named him Jacob."** (Genesis 25:26)

**"'This time I will praise the Lord.' Therefore she named him Judah."** (Genesis 29:35)

**"She named him Moses, explaining, I drew him out of the water."** (Exodus 2:10)

**"She bore a son and she named him Solomon."** (II Samuel, 12:24)

**"As for your wife Sarai, you shall not call her Sarai, but her name shall be Sarah."** (Genesis 17:15)

| | | | |
|---|---|---|---|
| Moses | מֹשֶׁה | עָקֵב | heel |
| Solomon | שְׁלֹמֹה | מְשִׁיתִהוּ | I drew him out |
| Jacob | יַעֲקֹב | חַי | living |
| Eve | חַוָּה | אוֹדֶה | I will praise |
| Judah | יְהוּדָה | שָׁלוֹם | peace |
| Sarah | שָׂרָה | שָׂרָה | princess |

Your full Hebrew name includes not just your Hebrew name, but the Hebrew names of your parents, too. Practice writing your full Hebrew name:

*For a Girl*

_____ bat _____ v' _____

(my Hebrew name) daughter of (my father's Hebrew name) and (my mother's Hebrew name)

*For a Boy*

_____ ben _____ v' _____

(my Hebrew name) son of (my father's Hebrew name) and (my mother's Hebrew name)

## Your Turn

Do you know what your Hebrew name means? Why were you given this name? Are you named after a family member, or is your name taken from the Bible? Write what you know about your Hebrew name and then research its meaning. If you don't know your Hebrew name or its origins, ask your family members about what you were named and why. Then make a sign for your room that includes your Hebrew name and symbols that reflect its meaning.

# This Child's Life

As you grow up, you will learn and try many new things. Not only do you have your friends and family by your side to help you, but you also have a guidebook for life—the Torah.

## Parents Blessing Children

Your parents wish the best for you and try to raise you to be a good person. It has been a custom since biblical times to give children blessings, wishing them a great future.

Jacob blessed his grandsons Manasseh and Ephraim, and so in many Jewish families, parents give their children this blessing on Shabbat, praying that they follow in the footsteps of Jewish leaders Manasseh and Ephraim and the four matriarchs.

Blessing for a son: *May God make you like Ephraim and Manasseh.*

Blessing for a daughter: *May God make you like Sarah, Rebecca, Rachel, and Leah.*

Blessing given by Jewish parents to their children: *May God bless you and protect you. May God shine the light of God's face upon you and give you grace. May God turn God's face towards you and give you peace.*

What do you think it means to follow in the footsteps of Jewish leaders of the past?

List four qualities of a Jewish leader, then circle one that you might follow.

1. _____    2. _____

3. _____    4. _____

### Talk about It

How does your Hebrew name add to your Jewish identity?

What other ways can you think of to make religious school "sweet" for new students?

# The Best Guide

Before you are expected to keep any mitzvot, you have to learn about them first. This leads us to the most basic mitzvah—learning Torah! But there is a lot to learn, so parents and teachers carefully choose what to teach Jewish students first.

> **At five years the age is reached for the study of the Torah, at ten for the study of Mishnah [collection of rabbinic laws], at thirteen for keeping the commandments, at fifteen for the study of the Talmud [collection of Jewish law, tradition, and teachings]...** (Pirkei Avot 5:24-25)

The sages of the Talmud recommended that the Bible be taught to young children and Jewish law be studied as they got older. Do you remember when you learned your first Bible story?

Which story was it? _____

What Jewish topics have you learned or do you think you will learn at different times in your life?

When I was 5: _____

When I am 13: _____

By the time I am 30: _____

By the time I am 50: _____

# A Sweet Start

Although you will learn a lot from those around you, you also go to school to get an education. Some Jewish communities have a special tradition on the first day of school. A teacher spreads honey over the Hebrew letters written on a small board, then asks a child to read the letters. When the answer is correct, the child licks off the honey. That way, the child's first memories of school are delicious and sweet.

What do you remember about your first day of religious school? _____

_____

# CHAPTER 5

# PREPARING TO BE A JEWISH ADULT

**Do you remember what it was like to be a toddler? What is the best thing now about being a kid? Each stage of life brings something new and exciting with it. Your childhood will end in one of the most important events of your life, your bar or bat mitzvah. Why is this time in your life so important?**

## Practice Makes Perfect

When you are young, you start keeping some Jewish traditions, such as celebrating Jewish holidays and giving tzedakah. You are still a Jew-in-training, and doing mitzvot at a young age is good practice for when you become a Jewish adult.

*Bar mitzvah* literally means "son of the commandment" and *bat mitzvah* literally means "daughter of the commandment." This is the age when you are old enough to take responsibility for your own decisions and to make sure that you keep the mitzvot. A boy reaches bar mitzvah at age thirteen, on his Hebrew birthday. Depending on the Jewish community, a girl will celebrate becoming a bat mitzvah at age twelve or thirteen.

## What to Do, What Not to Do

There are 613 mitzvot in the Torah. These mitzvot can be divided into positive and negative categories. Positive mitzvot are action-based, like giving tzedakah or honoring your parents. Negative mitzvot are based on not doing something, like not stealing. Rabbi

Joseph Karo, the sixteenth-century author of one of the most widely used books of Jewish law, advised parents to teach children the positive mitzvot first. Why do you think he recommended this approach? Do you agree with his approach?

## Dos and Don'ts

Of the 613 mitzvot in the Torah, 248 are positive mitzvot and 365 are negative mitzvot. According to the Talmud, these numbers are significant. The number 248 relates to the number of a person's limbs and body parts, while the number 365 is the number of days in a solar year. What do you think the connection is between mitzvot, our bodies, and time?

## Positive or Negative?

Identify the positive and negative commandments in the list below by writing **P** for Positive or **N** for Negative next to each one.

Eat matzah on Passover. _____

Study the Torah. _____

Do not hold a grudge. _____

Rest on Shabbat. _____

Do not destroy a Torah scroll. _____

Do not eat on Yom Kippur. _____

Believe in one God. _____

Do not tell tales. _____

Hear the shofar on Rosh Hashanah. _____

Say the Sh'ma prayer. _____

Do not curse your parents. _____

## Pointing in the Right Direction

When you were a baby learning to walk, your parents probably helped you until you could make it on your own. So too, as you take the steps that prepare you for your bar or bat mitzvah milestone, you get guidance from your family and teachers. But finally, the time will come for you to stand on your own. The bar or bat mitzvah ceremony marks this change. A central part of the ceremony, the receiving of an *aliyah* (saying the blessings over the reading of the Torah), celebrates your new status as a Jewish adult. Now, along with the rest of the Jewish community, it is your job to study the Torah and act according to its teachings.

# Preparing for the Big Day

In some ways, you prepare for becoming bar or bat mitzvah from a very young age, as you are developing your Jewish identity. But the practical preparations begin in the year or two before your bar or bat mitzvah day arrives. Boys and girls have a lot of options for their ceremony. Many read from the Torah, recite prayers, and give a speech. There's often a party and a mitzvah project. All of these aspects of the ceremony take careful preparation. Decisions about the celebration itself can take a lot of time too.

# Reading the Parashah

The ceremony is held at a time when the public Torah reading takes place, usually in the synagogue on Shabbat morning. A boy or girl may read part or all of the week's *parashah*, Torah portion, or *Haftarah*, the related selection from the Prophets.

## Meet Jacopo

**Lives in: Milan, Italy**

**My Greatest Challenge:** The hardest thing I've ever done is prepare for my bar mitzvah. I spent one weekend every month in Venice [Italy] in order to study my parashah, *Lech Lecha*, with my teacher. After I completed my reading on the day of my bar mitzvah, I felt wonderful, but also sad that it was over.

**Favorite Biblical Story:** *Lech Lecha*, because I read it on my bar mitzvah. It talks about Abraham leaving his land for Israel. I feel that this parashah represents my family because we travel a lot.

**Best Bar Mitzvah Gift:** I have one object that I am attached to because it was a bar mitzvah gift from my grandparents—a Mont Blanc pen. I love writing, and this pen seems to almost magically give me ideas. This is the pen I used to write my first book about my life, which I wrote for a school project and even managed to get published. I hope in the future to keep writing.

# What Are They Thinking?

What do you think each person is thinking or feeling during a bar or bat mitzvah ceremony? Fill in the bubbles with each person's thoughts about this sacred time.

Her father

Her mother

Her sister

The Bat Mitzvah

# One Mitzvah Follows Another

Many boys and girls also choose to give back to the community as part of their preparation, giving them a chance to explore one of the many mitzvot related to *g'milut ḥasadim*, acts of kindness. Called mitzvah projects, these efforts are tailored to the personal interests of the bar mitzvah boy or bat mitzvah girl. Collecting and donating toys to a children's hospital, volunteering in a soup kitchen, or reading to the elderly are all examples of mitzvah projects. Some choose to do a tzedakah project, raising money for a favorite cause. Often the project is mentioned in the **d'var Torah**, the speech a boy or girl gives at the bar or bat mitzvah celebration.

# Pay It Forward

Doing acts of *g'milut ḥasadim* can have a ripple effect in the world, as more and more people are affected by acts of kindness, and in turn, do the same for others. A mitzvah project does this by teaching others about a community need and addressing it.

Think of whom you would like to help with your mitzvah project and the ripple effects your project could have. Complete a chain of events for your mitzvah project idea below.

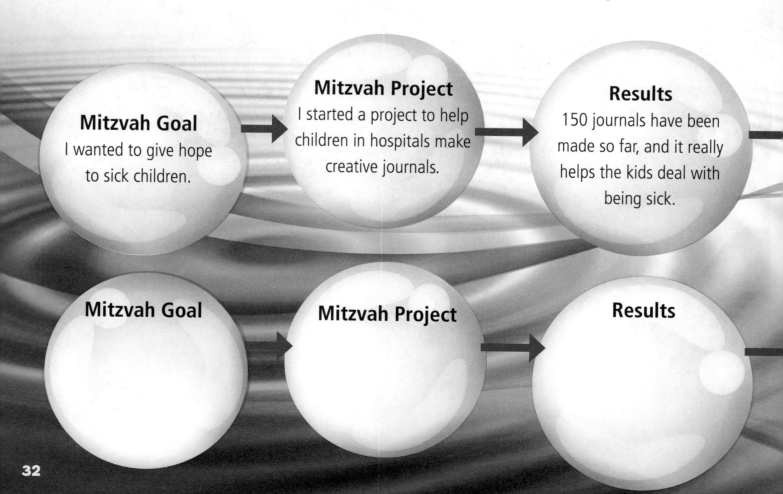

**Mitzvah Goal**
I wanted to give hope to sick children.

**Mitzvah Project**
I started a project to help children in hospitals make creative journals.

**Results**
150 journals have been made so far, and it really helps the kids deal with being sick.

**Mitzvah Goal**

**Mitzvah Project**

**Results**

# A Lifelong Commitment

After your bar or bat mitzvah, you are a full-fledged member of the Jewish nation, and you still have the Torah as your ultimate guide. As one ancient sage said about the Torah, "Turn it again and again, for everything is in it."

Many students choose to continue their formal Jewish education after their bar or bat mitzvah. In some congregations, when students are fifteen or sixteen, they have another Jewish celebration, called the **confirmation** ceremony. Usually held on the holiday of Shavuot, confirmation is a kind of graduation ceremony when the whole class confirms their commitment to the Torah, as the Israelites did as a group at Mount Sinai.

## Words to Know:
### S'udat Mitzvah

Another highlight of the bar and bat mitzvah event is when everyone comes together to celebrate! Even eating is a mitzvah at this time. In fact, the festive meal at many bar and bat mitzvah parties is called a **s'udat mitzvah**.

## Talk about It

How can you continue your Jewish learning after your bar or bat mitzvah? How can a mitzvah project be turned into a lifetime commitment to doing *g'milut ḥasadim*?

### Ripple Effect

Kids are passing on the idea and sharing their journals, giving other sick kids hope.

### Ripple Effect

# CHAPTER 6

# ESTABLISHING A JEWISH HOME

Jewish life isn't only about what you do in religious school or at the synagogue. Jewish life begins at home, with you and your family. How many mitzvot can you think of that you do right at home? What would you expect to see in a Jewish home?

## Family Beginnings

Home is where the people you love are—your family. You, too, can look forward to building your own home and family one day.

A wedding is a way for two people to begin a family. There are many special rituals and customs at Jewish weddings that make it a meaningful and joyous event. A **ḥatunah**, a Jewish wedding, celebrates the personal happiness of the families in the wedding party and the community-wide happiness over the continuity of Am Yisrael. Memories of this event are treasured and tell the story of a family's beginning.

## Pages from a Jewish Wedding Album

Friends and family watch as the **kalah**, the bride, walks down the aisle to meet her **ḥatan**, groom. The ḥatan and kalah are often escorted down the aisle by their parents.

The ḥatan and kalah meet under the **ḥupah**, the wedding canopy. Usually made from fabric, and sometimes just a tallit, the ḥupah symbolizes the new home the couple will build.

34

The wedding ceremony has two main parts, **kiddushin** and **nisu'in**. The rabbi begins the kiddushin part of the ceremony with two blessings, including one over a cup of wine, from which the couple each take a sip. The groom places a ring on the bride's finger. At some weddings, the bride also gives the groom a ring. The rings are usually made of gold.

Next, the **k'tubah**, Jewish marriage contract, is read aloud. The k'tubah, whose name comes from the Hebrew word "to write," is often written in the finest calligraphy and beautifully decorated. Some of the main items included in a traditional k'tubah are the names of the bride and groom, date and place of the wedding, the groom's proposal and its acceptance by the bride, and a promise from the groom to take care of his new wife. It is signed by two witnesses.

The second part of the wedding ceremony is the **nisu'in**, which consists of seven blessings thanking God for Creation and for bringing the couple together. The ḥatan and kalah sip from a second cup of wine, and then the ḥatan stamps on a glass to break it. The broken glass reminds us that, even at our happiest moment, we remember the destruction of the Temple in Jerusalem. The guests then greet the new married couple with cheers of "*Mazal Tov! Congratulations!*"

The celebration continues, with plenty of food and a lot of dancing. It is a mitzvah for the wedding guests to entertain the ḥatan and kalah, even juggling for their entertainment.

# Royalty for a Day

For just one day, the bride and groom are treated like a king and queen. They are the center of attention, and all efforts are made to keep them happy and to make sure that every part of the wedding runs smoothly. Every detail of the wedding, from the bride's outfit to the festive meal, is meant to make this day an outstanding memory for the happy couple.

# Wedding Help

A lot goes on at a Jewish wedding. Imagine that you are the wedding planner and you have to arrange all the necessary items for each part of the wedding. Match the correct item to each activity for which it is needed. Keep in mind that some items are used for more than one step.

Signing the k'tubah

Wedding procession

Kiddushin

Nisu'in

Saying Sheva B'rachot

Reading the k'tubah

Photo session

S'udat mitzvah

Wedding dances

Grace After Meals

# What the Bride Wore

Today most American Jewish brides wear white wedding dresses. In some Jewish communities, however, the tradition was for the bride to wear a beautiful, colorful outfit that made her the center of attention. A Yemenite bride's costume involved the whole community; everyone lent the bride different items in order that she look her best.

### Words to Know:
### Sheva B'rachot

The seven blessings said under the ḥupah are called **Sheva B'rachot** in Hebrew. In some communities, friends and family continue to rejoice with the ḥatan and kalah for the whole week after the wedding. The Sheva B'rachot are said during Birkat Hamazon, Grace After Meals, at each of these parties.

# Meet Leora

**Lives in:  Highland Park, New Jersey**

*When Leora's father remarried, Leora and her sister were junior bridesmaids at the wedding.*

**What It Was Like:** We held bouquets just like the bride's, but miniature ones. I was nervous beforehand, but it was fun. We walked down the aisle to the ḥupah and stood next to my grandmother. When the glass was broken, I jumped because I was zoning out and then suddenly I heard the crack. After the ḥupah, there was a meal and dancing. We even had a hula hoop competition.

**Best Wedding Memory:** My cousin lined us up by the door and gave us arches covered in flowers to hold up, for my mom and dad to walk under when they came into the party room. We were waiting for about ten minutes, so my arms got tired!

## Turning a House into a Jewish Home

The Jewish community welcomes each new Jewish household with joy. The wedding is just the beginning, and families grow quickly. Every Jewish family has its special place in Am Yisrael, the Jewish community. Each family has its own unique story to tell. What's your family's tale?

## A Blessed House

Jewish homes have a unique item on their doorposts, the mezuzah. This Hebrew word actually means "doorpost" but refers to a small scroll on which the first two paragraphs of the Sh'ma are written. The mezuzah reminds us, as we leave and enter our houses, to live a life that reflects Jewish values and beliefs. When you see a mezuzah on someone's door, you know that it is a Jewish home, and this sign connects you to other families in Am Yisrael.

## Your Turn

Create a diagram that portrays your family, such as a family tree or links in a chain. You may include only your immediate family or add more family members. What symbol will you use to represent your family? What makes your family different and special?

## Design in Reach

The mezuzah scroll is protected with a mezuzah cover, often beautifully decorated. The Hebrew letter *shin* usually appears on the cover. Design your own mezuzah cover here with symbols that represent your family and your favorite mitzvot. Make sure to include the Hebrew letter *shin* in your design.

## Give a Little Respect

You may not be an adult yet, but you can have a hand in giving your home a Jewish flavor. Respecting our parents and making guests feel welcome are both mitzvot that improve the atmosphere in our homes. In fact, it is even a mitzvah to keep things peaceful between family members, such as between siblings. This is known as *sh'lom bayit*.

What are some specific things you can do to give your home a Jewish flavor?

1. _____

2. _____

3. _____

### Talk about It

What does it mean to you to have a Jewish home? What makes your house a Jewish home?

# CHAPTER 7

# MOURNING A LOSS THE JEWISH WAY

**Jewish tradition teaches us that saving a life is like saving an entire world. Human life is precious, and we are taught to appreciate each person in this world. How can we show our respect for each and every human life? Why do you think we consider each life to be "an entire world"?**

## Valuing Life

Even though we do everything we can to save lives and heal people, we can't stop death completely. Death is a natural part of the human life cycle. When we suffer the loss of a person close to us, Jewish tradition helps us honor their memories and express our sadness through the process of Jewish mourning. Although the loss of those we love is very painful, we are helped by having the support of our friends and family and our Jewish traditions.

## Giving It Time

Jewish tradition recognizes how hard it is to lose someone. Special rituals for *aveilut*, mourning, give family members a way to express their grief. Different periods in the mourning process were established to help mourners, slowly but surely, cope with their loss. Each stage in the mourning process consists of its own rituals and customs.

## The First Days

A Jewish funeral is usually held as soon as possible after a person's death. Out of respect for the one who has passed away, the body is never left alone;

someone is with the body at all times until it is buried. Jewish funerals are kept simple and focus on honoring the memory of the loved one. Mourners tear a piece of their clothing or wear a torn black ribbon as a way of expressing their grief. Speeches called eulogies are given that describe the deceased and his or her special qualities.

## The Week After

After the funeral, family members "sit *shiva*" for up to a week (*shiva* means "seven," referring to a period of seven days). This means that the family members mourn together in one of their homes, and do not participate in their usual activities, such as going to work. Mourners traditionally sit on low stools and cover all the mirrors in their homes so as to focus on their mourning instead of on how they look. Friends visit to give comfort and share their good memories of the person who passed away. Prayer services are held in the shiva house too.

## A Month Passes

After the shiva period, mourners begin to return to their regular routines but continue to observe some laws of mourning and say special prayers. This month is called **sh'loshim**, which means "thirty," referring to the number of days in an average month.

### Giving Comfort

One common custom when leaving a shiva house is to say to the mourners:

"May God comfort you among all the mourners of Zion and Jerusalem."

## A Year Goes By

Each stage of mourning is less intense than the one before it, reflecting how our emotions calm with time. For most mourners, the end of the sh'loshim period means a return to daily life even though they still feel a loss. But for one mourning for a parent, the whole year is a year of grieving. A child says a prayer, the **Kaddish**, in memory of a father or mother, and some continue to observe mourning laws such as not attending parties.

At the end of the year, many families return to the cemetery for the unveiling service, when the gravestone is set in place at the gravesite. This marks the end of the mourning time, even though a person's memory stays with you forever.

# Keeping Memories Alive

Even after the official time to mourn ends, we continue to remember our loved ones who have died. One tradition is to light a memorial candle on the **yahrtzeit**, the anniversary of their death. Some people also visit the grave, leaving a stone on it as a sign that they remembered. In addition, a special memorial service called **Yizkor** is said on major Jewish holidays in the synagogue to honor the memory of those who have died.

Another way to memorialize people we care about is by naming children after them. Do you know of anyone in your family who is named after an ancestor?

# A Sign for Eternity

How can you tell that the cemetery in the photo to the right is a Jewish cemetery? What Jewish signs and symbols do you notice? Why do you think they are included on the tombstones?

# The Cave at Machpelah

Our ancestors taught us by example to show respect for people after they die. Abraham himself went to great lengths to find a place in which to bury Sarah. Called Ma'arat Hamachpelah, the cave at Machpelah, it also became the burial place of our forefathers and foremothers Abraham, Sarah, Isaac, Rebecca, Jacob, and Leah. Today, many people still visit this spot in Hebron to honor their memories.

# The Whole Community Remembers

Just as our community comes together to celebrate joyous occasions, we also join together to commemorate losses that affected all the Jewish people, like on Yom Hashoah, Holocaust Memorial Day. There are many ways in which we remember these tragedies together. We have mourning rituals and special ceremonies that help us mark the dark times in Jewish history.

## Mourning the Temple

One of the oldest communal memorial days is Tisha B'Av, the ninth day of the Hebrew month of Av, the day on which both Temples in Jerusalem were destroyed. It is traditional to fast on Tisha B'Av and to observe other customs of mourning as well. On this day, many also recall other tragedies that happened to Am Yisrael. In the synagogue, we read Lamentations, the portion of the *Tanach* that describes the destruction of the first Temple. Even the tune for reading Lamentations is slow and sad.

**Talk about It**

What events from Jewish history do you think are important to commemorate? What are other ways you can think of to honor the memory of a loved one?

# CHAPTER 8

# THIS JEWISH LIFE

Judaism helps us pay attention to the passing of time, so that we make the most of every precious minute of our lives. Now that you have learned how time counts in Jewish life, take a trip along the road of your life. You can't predict what the future will bring, but you can use Jewish values to guide your life course.

## Object of the Game:

Make it through all the Jewish life-cycle events and collect points by answering questions and making decisions. Try to collect as many points as possible by game's end.

## How to Play:

1. Make your own game piece by folding a small piece of paper as shown and sketching yourself on one side.

2. Personalize the game board by drawing in your house, family, and friends in the spaces provided.

3. Place your game piece on the Start space.

4. Travel around the game board, following the instructions on each space.

5. Circle the points you earn as you advance around the board and add them up at the end. See if you can earn 365 points!

**Getting Started**

**Life Cycle START**
You are born! Receive 10 points for being a bundle of joy.
*move 1 ahead*

**Adventure**
Come home from the hospital and meet your family! Gain 5 points.
*move 1 ahead*

**Life Cycle**
Celebrate your brit milah or brit/simhat bat. Gain 25 points.
*move 1 ahead*

**Torah Talk**
You get your Hebrew name. Receive 10 points if your name is biblical.
*move 1 ahead*

**Growing Up**

**Torah Talk**
You hear your first biblical story about an ark and a flood. Collect 10 points.
*move 1 ahead*

**Mitzvah Day**
Eat your first Shabbat dinner with your family. Gain 10 points.
*move 1 ahead*

**Make a Choice**
Start religious school. If you know the Hebrew word for teacher, gain 15 points and move ahead 2 spaces. If not, move ahead 1 space.

**Adventure**
Fall asleep during synagogue services. Lose 5 points.
*move 1 ahead*

44

## Becoming an Adult

**Mitzvah Day**
Fast for the first time on Yom Kippur. Gain 15 points.

**Make a Choice**
Do you continue in Hebrew high school after your bar/bat mitzvah? If yes, collect 25 points and advance 1 space. If no, move ahead 2 spaces.

**Draw your house here.**

**Life Cycle**
Celebrate your confirmation! Receive 25 points.

**Life Cycle**
Your bar/bat mitzvah goes off without a hitch! Collect 50 points for reading your Torah portion, giving your d'var Torah, and hosting a great party.

**Adventure**
Go to Jewish summer camp. Gain 15 points.

**Mitzvah Day**
For your mitzvah project, you help a worthy cause. Gain 30 points.

**Make a Choice**
It is time to go to college and choose a career. What profession will you choose? Name one mitzvah related to your profession. Then collect 15 points.

**Torah Talk**
You study your Torah portion well. Gain 30 points.

**Adventure**
Miss a session with your bar mitzvah tutor because you overslept. Lose 5 points.

**Life Cycle**
Mazal tov on your Jewish wedding! Receive 50 points. Add a spouse to your game piece.

**Make a Choice**
Will you learn to read your haftarah? If no, advance 2 spaces. If yes, collect 25 points and advance 1 space.

## Adult Life

## Bar/Bat Mitzvah Time

**Adventure**
Celebrate your sheva b'rachot, then fly to Israel for your honeymoon. Gain 5 points.

**Make a Choice**
Schedule conflict: Do you pay a shiva visit or attend a concert? If you choose the shiva, gain 15 points and move ahead 1 space. If you choose the concert, move ahead two spaces.

**Mitzvah Day**
Buy a house and affix a mezuzah to each doorpost. Collect 15 points if you remember the prayer written in the mezuzah scroll.

**Draw your family and friends here.**

**Mitzvah Day**
Host your family and in-laws for a Passover seder. Gain 15 points.

**Life Cycle**
Mazal tov! You have twins—a girl and a boy! Receive 50 points. Add them to your game piece, invite friends and family to the brit milah and brit bat.

**Torah Talk**
Teach your children Torah. Name 3 biblical stories. Collect 5 points for each answer.

**Turn to page 46 to tally your points.**

# Taking Stock

There's no retiring from Torah and mitzvot. Take stock of your life and tally your points.

How many points do you have?_____

How can you keep increasing them in real life? _____

How can you teach your children to live their lives, too, according to Jewish time? _____

_____

# Staying Centered

As you go through different times in life, it is helpful to have a solid core and a strong Jewish identity. How can you achieve this?

Complete this Magen David by writing your top Jewish times in the middle. Then, in the corners of the star, write the people, places, books, and anything else that are a part of these times.

**My Jewish Time**

What makes some Jewish events the top ones in your life? _____

_____

Who and what best help you keep "Jewish time"? _____

_____

How can you plan to have more good times in the future? _____

_____

How does the Jewish idea of time build your Jewish identity? _____

_____

# Checklist

Give yourself a big check mark for each of the Your Turn experiences you have tried.

☐ Add a verse of your own to King Solomon's words, page 7

☐ Create a chart with sketches of the cycles of the moon, page 15

☐ Discover the meaning of your Hebrew name and make a sign for your name, page 25

☐ Design a diagram that represents your family, page 38

What other Jewish experiences have you tried for the first time this year?

✔ _____

✔ _____

✔ _____

# WORDS TO KNOW

**Am Yisrael**    Hebrew for "the people of Israel;" the worldwide Jewish community.

**b'rachah**    Hebrew for "blessing."

**bar mitzvah**    Hebrew for "son of the commandment;" a thirteen-year-old boy who is now responsible for fulfilling God's commandments (mitzvot).

**bat mitzvah**    Hebrew for "daughter of the commandment;" a twelve-year-old or thirteen-year-old girl who is now responsible for fulfilling God's commandments (mitzvot).

**ḥupah**    The wedding canopy under which a Jewish bride (**kalah**) and groom (**ḥatan**) stand during the marriage ceremony (**ḥatunah**).

**Kiddush**    From the Hebrew word *kadosh*, which means "holy;" blessings said on Shabbat over wine or grape juice to sanctify the holy day.

**Rosh Hashanah**    Hebrew for "head of the year;" a major Jewish holiday celebrated on the first two days of the new Jewish year.

**Rosh Ḥodesh**    Hebrew for "head of the month;" a minor Jewish holiday celebrated at the beginning of each new Jewish month.

**sacred**    Holy or set apart.

**Shabbat**    Hebrew for "rest;" the final day of Creation; the Jewish Sabbath, celebrated from Friday evening until Saturday evening.

**shavu'a**    From the Hebrew word *sheva*, which means "seven;" a week.

**shiva**    The seven-day mourning period that begins after a funeral.